Heart-Strapped

Heart-Strapped

A Widow's Journey through Grief

Nikki Kirk

RESOURCE *Publications* · Eugene, Oregon

HEART-STRAPPED
A Widow's Journey through Grief

Resource Publications
An Imprint of Wipf and Stock Publishers
199 W. 8th Ave., Suite 3
Eugene, OR 97401

www.wipfandstock.com

PAPERBACK ISBN: 978-1-7252-8488-3
HARDCOVER ISBN: 978-1-7252-8486-9
EBOOK ISBN: 978-1-7252-8489-0

03/02/21

For Fraser

The contents of this book contain subject matter relating to suicide, depression, mental health, and grief.

Please practice self-care during and after reading.

If you are in crisis, please phone:
Canada
Crisis Services Canada: 1–833-456–4566 or Text 45645
Connect with a Crisis Counselor: Text "HOME" to 741741

United States
Suicide Prevention Lifeline: 1–800-273–8255 or 1–800-784–2433
Connect with a Crisis Counselor: Text "HOME" to 741741

United Kingdom
HopeLine UK: 0800 068 4141
Samaritans Helpline: 116 123
Connect with a Crisis Counselor: Text "HOME" to 85258

The author would like to acknowledge that a part of the proceeds of this book will go to supporting the Canadian Suicide Prevention Service also known as Crisis Service Canada.

Crisis Service Canada offers a barrier-free, non-judgmental space with supportive and responsive responders. Their free and confidential services are available 24 hours, 7 days a week.

For additional information on this organization go to:
www.crisisservicecanada.ca

CONTENTS

ACKNOWLEDGMENTS

THE COMPLETION OF THIS book would not have been possible without the love and support of my family—Mom, Dad, Nathan, and Amanda. Thank you for accompanying me in the valleys and always keeping a light on to find my way home in the darkest days of grief.

To my mom, Jana, your incomparable support and profound belief in my work kept me going when I wanted to scrap the entire project. You always had faith in my abilities, for that I have the utmost gratitude.

I am also truly grateful for the support of Fraser's family—Tricia, John, and Laura. You are beautiful souls with hearts of pure gold. Your love is greatly felt.

I cannot begin to express my thanks to Sarah Schnieders, who was able to take my wild ideas and create gorgeous line art illustrations to accompany my poetry. How you turned my awkward rough sketches into something beautiful, I will never know. You are a magician.

I would like to express my deepest appreciation to the team at Wipf and Stock. Particularly, George, Matthew, Emily, Zechariah, and Rachel. Your patience and dedication cannot be underestimated.

I would like to extend my deepest gratitude to the beautiful friends that walked beside me through my grief—Jasmine, Sylvia, Emily, and Eden. You helped me to find joy again. I will be forever grateful for your unwavering love.

Finally, to my love, Fraser, thank you for the years of beautiful memories. We had a lifetime of love in only a handful of years. I was blessed to call you mine for the time you were here.

PROLOGUE

I WAS TWENTY-EIGHT WHEN my husband died by suicide. It was a Friday night in November during a snowstorm. I remember waiting for him to come home from work. Waiting, waiting, and waiting. Then a phone call. It was him. He would be working late at the office and bring home dinner. Half an hour turned into an hour, turned into two. When my phone finally buzzed, I leapt over the kitchen counter, seizing it in my already shaky hands. It was him. One text. Telling me goodbye. Telling me to take care of our dog. Telling me that he will always love me. Telling me where to find his body. Four sentences laced up in love and dragging me into hell.

We had built a life together over the last seven years. We bought our first home just the summer before and furnished it with treasures that we had collected on our adventures around the world. We were planning on starting a family of our own in the new year and let our excitement carry us away in dreaming of the great escapades we would have together. Life was everything it was meant to be, but the messages inside his head told him otherwise.

The suicide was blindsiding. It was difficult to comprehend what had happened, and to realize that he was not going to be coming back home. I spent weeks waiting by the front door for him to return from work, listening for the familiar sound of the garage opening, and preparing for the nightmare to cease. It never did end.

The first couple of years without him were excruciating to live. Night and day slipped into one another; nightmares blurring with the terrors I experienced during the daylight. Despite the unrelenting agony, there was one thing that I knew, one thing that I still had the resolve to do: I was not going to let my late husband's monsters become my own. I would not let the waves of grief drown me, as I knew was frighteningly possible. I fought. I tread. I swam. I eventually learned how to create a façade of forward movement—getting up, showering, going out, and coming home. My heart ultimately followed and I made incremental steps forward. I went back to work, I started to see my friends again, and I began looking towards the future. In the years that followed, the grief was not lesser, but I was stronger.

Today, I am still healing, still grieving, and still moving forward. Yet, I am far closer to the life that my late husband and I dreamt of, but I had to forge that life on my own. With blisters on my hands, and callouses on my feet, I journey forth on a path that I never thought I would find myself on. I am learning to find moments of joy along the way, and gratitude in the voyage.

ORGANIZATION OF COLLECTION

THIS COLLECTION OF POETRY is organized into seasons—beginning in the bitter gales of winter and ending in the colorful spell of autumn. The poetry follows the trajectory of my grief. The first section is heavy and drips with pain and misery. In spring, the darkness of denial begins to melt and the dark underbelly of grief is exposed. Summer makes way for the dissolution of grief fog, but exhaustion and the prickly remnants of heartache remain. Alas, autumn arrives and the possibilities of new life shake me awake and I am ready to move forward, taking my late husband's memory with me as I tread onward into a new life.

Part I

WINTER

FLUTTER

We made our bed out of the breath of dandelions
Floating on the summer winds

Making promises that would take a lifetime to keep

Creating dreams from the remnants
Of the little boy and little girl still living within us
Tying them to the wings of the blackbird
Watching them take flight

I peeled off the exoskeleton that bound my hopes
Placed it in your hands
When it hit your palms, it turned to ash

You whispered
"You don't need this anymore"
Then you wrapped your arms around me
Squeezing tightly
Until the pieces that were trapped inside
Under the layers of insecurity and pain
Rose to the surface

I grew wings that day

Then you left
Clipping my feathers
Binding me to the earth
When my home was in the skies

BITTERSWEET

I have tasted death
She lingers in my mouth
Bitter like the tang of charred meat

       I drink tonics
       That promise me freedom
       From the heartache that has made
       Its home inside my veins

   My blood still runs black
   Like the night that you fled
   We burned the body that you left behind
   The flames reducing a man to powder

       My heart emerges from the drunken sea
       Gulping down the thought of you at peace

Softly sleeping among the gods
Dancing wildly among the crimson stars

       You are home
         Yes, I know

       Though, my dear, you were my home

CLEMENCY

I hate that my heart has chosen to beat on without you
There should be a rule
Unspoken
That when one soulmate's heart loses its beat
Its twin should too come to a rest

Call it the law of compassion

GHOULS

The sorrow waits for me
Trapped inside the chest where I hid it
Multiplying until it has nowhere to go
Only to escape from my pores
The stench of it curdling the air wherever I roam

Words unspoken coat my tongue
I walk through minefields masquerading as magic
Ghouls and goblins patrol the bridge towards the day
When I can begin again

HUSH-HUSH

The hypnotic tempo of life
Was just reaching its crescendo
Before halting
I sit in the silence that you created for me

    The quiet destroys me

OBEDIENCE

Yesterday you were a pinprick
A small thorn buried under my skin
A paracetamol was all that was needed
To dull the pain

> Today you are Meningitis, Smallpox, Ebola
> A plane crash and a burning house
> Brooding. Bloody. Bruising.

You demand my attention
Like a small child screaming for my love

"Look at me!" "See me!" "Feel me!"

> Even now, after months have passed
> Birthdays. Anniversaries. Holidays.
> Coming. Lingering. Leaving.

> You are still here

> You still come in and call to me
> Like a monsoon I cannot run from
> You fill the places in my mind
> That I have cleared for something new

"I am here." "Feel me."

> Like an obedient child
> I do

SOAP & WATER

Sorrow sits under my fingernails
I wash my hands
Scrubbing
Scraping
Until droplets of blood rise to the surface

And still
My soul wails for you

LAUNDRY DAY

Slit my wrists
Tear my lungs from my chest
Strip my bones of marrow

Pull out my veins
Use them as a noose

Tug out my heart

String up my organs
Hang them out with the wash
Let the neighbors see

All I want
Is to remove the parts
That keep me from you

COUNTDOWN

How much longer until we are reunited?
Hours, even minutes, are too long
I can only bear a few seconds without you

10, 9, 8
I can hardly wait
7, 6, 5, 4
Only a few more
3, 2, 1
Is it done?

I wait

You are not here
I am not there
The disappointment is a raging wildfire
Burning through my heart

Alas
I start again
10, 9, 8 . . .

JUDAS

Each day that I awake
without you
sleeping next to me
is another betrayal from God.

WINTERTIDE

I used to hear church bells
In the first snowflake
That fell from the sky

        Smell Christmas morning
        In the brisk autumn breeze
        That made me reach for my scarf

Now all that I can smell
Is the rot and decay
Of the fermenting earth

        Hear the muffled screams of leaves
        As the snow blankets the ground
        Smothering what little hope I had left

"Winter is too long to be without you," I whisper

And no one hears

NIGHTFALL

Since you left
Even the sun
Can no longer resist
The shifting night

SLUMBER

When my demons go to sleep
I do the things that I could not do
When they ruled and raged
But their slumber never lasts

They awaken
And I drown again

WRATH

We walk together towards the springs of old age
Carrying only our memories tucked deep into our pockets
You hold my hand and hum Vivaldi's Autumn
You must have known that winter was coming

I kneel down
My knees skim the roots of the white birch rising around us
I pluck a strawberry growing wild upon the path
I smile knowing that it is your favorite

As I stand, I search for you
Cradling the berry in my palm
You are gone
I call your name
You do not answer

I squish the soft berry in my hand
Its bloody pulp runs between my fingers
Spilling to the rough earth below

I smear the remaining flesh and seeds on my face
Screaming until the robins have left their nests
And the ants flee back to their colonies underground

      The forest floor shakes with my fury
      Heaven knows I will destroy the world with my pain

BONES

The loneliness creeps into everything
Invading each muscle
Carving its way into my bloodstream

I weep tears of abandonment
That pool on my sunken cheeks

At night I want to make bad choices
To do anything that will remove the sting
That loneliness has left inside my aching bones

DOLOR

Something as simple
as a good morning kiss

now taken

is my flesh and bones
exposed
to an angry world.

YAHWEH

A cocoon harshly ripped open
The caterpillar still inside
Growing, morphing
The nurturing waters spill out of the vessel
The caterpillar screaming
Writhing on its back
A half formed mutant

Monster
Demon

Exposed to a world it was not ready for
Mangled wings half formed
What cruel hand would do this?
Could it be true
That the same one who gave life
Has stripped it away

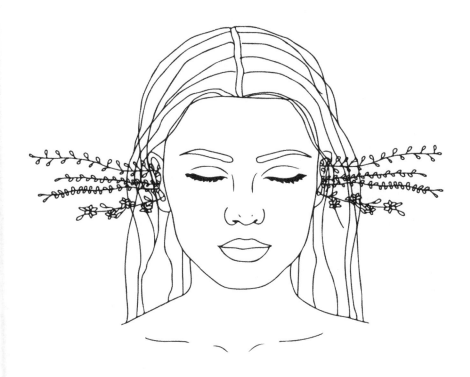

BALLAD

My grief-song is so loud
That sometimes
I cannot even hear
The sounds of the day

WITCHING HOURS

I feel you in the breath between sleeping and waking
You take my hand and we walk
Side by side, hip to hip, soul to soul

We follow the path that so many have walked before
You name all the rocks that crunch beneath our feet
I point out the wildflowers that line the forest floor
Your cherry red cheeks and broad smile reflect my own happy heartbeat

Then I awake

The stillness strangles my breath and I realize that I am alone
The heart that once beat beside me is now gone
I sit in the silence of my cold room until the agony finds me again
Rippling through my body
Filling each chord of my lifeless heart
The sorrow pulls at my soul and shreds it again

The night erases the memory of the pain
Sleep stitches back my spirit
Gently rocking my heart to sleep

Morning always comes

With it brings the heartache that will never let me go
I am forever damned by your betrayal of life
The promises you did not keep plaster my waking mind
Forbidding the light from peeking in

DECAY

They should have buried me with you
I have been a corpse since the day you left

Ninety percent rot and decay
Five percent human
Five percent hope

RUMINATION

Drifting on empty seas
Caught in a web
That stretches from one shore to another

Trapped in the middle of nothingness
With a ship full of memories
Stacked in wooden crates on the hull

Not even the stars shine out here
An unnerving quiet begins to settle
Like dust over the cracks in the ships frame

The waves lap up on the rotting boards
The craft shifts left, then right
Constantly moving, but going nowhere

I am the only passenger
Me and the crates
That keep me company in the night
Leaving splinters
Where I have grasped them fiercely

Clinging to their contents
Rather than looking for the shoreline

BASE COAT

Stomach churning
Tongue burning with last nights dinner
Coughing up memories of November

I cannot escape the pain
Or outrun the sorrow that drenches me
Coating every piece of skin

Hard bristles scraping my flesh
Blood mixing in with the grey
An unsightly medley of ash and blood

Now what is left
Is a blood-spattered canvas
Dripping in memories

COCOON

Twist my body into a cocoon
Snap my bones, tear my cartilage to make me fit
Peel back the skin that binds me together
Bury me in the ground where he lay

Let me rest there
Until he comes home

WANDERER

I am a lonely wanderer
Destined to walk through the mire and thicket
With only the hum of the land to guide me

Abandoned by all other nature
A foe to all beasts
I journey alone

Life has forgotten me
I have forgotten the fruits of her belly

I must keep pace
Or be demolished
By the grisly beasts of the woods

My breath matches
The rapid pace of my feet
Traveling until the earth
No longer burns beneath my soles

Only then
Will the dead carry me home

FLOAT

Melancholia drips down my legs
Staining my new summer dress
Spattering over my white suede heels

Its origin are these tiny holes
Sprayed across this empty heart
That still tremors every time I hear his name

I smear a thick plaster over the holes
Caulking and filling
The pain still bleeds through
A tireless fight that I do not know if I will ever win

Sometimes I put the tools down
Let the thick liquid pool around me
It rises swiftly
Covering my ruby painted toes and alabaster ankles

Ascending to the thighs that he once adored
Swirling around my hips before rising to my waist
Climbing hastily to my shoulders
Settling around my neck

Strangling me
Cutting off my supply to the tonic of life

I kick out my legs and flail my arms
Swimming in the pool of melancholia
When my legs begin to tire, I flip on to my back
Let the currents take me
Riding them through the night

I watch the stars flicker
Listen to the moon whisper her grave lullabies

FLAME

Put me out
like the flame of a candle.

Wet your fingers
and let me have peace.

HOUSE

The smell of death lingers here
A place that was once our home
Now is nothing more than wood and plaster

It has been weeks since you have been gone
Your spirit and flesh torn apart

I feel the hands of death tighten around my neck
I beg them to squeeze tighter
Constrict my life until I am on the otherside
They never do
They simply rest there, taunting me

"Take me! Take me!"
I cry out

Pleading with the space between you and me
The silence persists

Here I am
Alone
In a house that still smells of you

TAXES

Tax season is immeasurably tedious
When you are doing taxes for a dead man

First, he is reduced to ashy powder
Now, he is numbers scribbled on a lined page
      Facts
         Figures
Lines of data running into each other

The man I once built my coliseum with is gone
I am left with the raw data
Of everything he was
All that he had hoped to be
Spewed across official government documents

ABSURDITIES

You pull thorns from my flesh
Telling me
To be grateful
For the fragrance of the rose

1001

There were a thousand reasons to stay
You chose a thousand and one

Stopping *your* heart from aching
And starting *mine*

HEM

I sew tapestries
From the pain you left behind
Until my walls
Are filled with murals
Of a life that never was

Part II

SPRING

TIME

Time consumes
Your memory

I beg her
Leave a few more pieces

She is greedy
Taking your smile
Your heartbeat
Your touch

Now all that I can remember
Is the way you made me feel
When you left

KISS

Death kisses my cheek
Every time I think of you

I cannot stop
As even now
You are my favorite word

So, I let her kiss me
And shatter my heart once more

MAKE-BELIEF

I want to come home to you
After a day like this
When the world has shaken me
I want to curl into you

Counting the stars in your heartbeat
Listening to you share tales
Of princesses slaying the dragon

I can hear your words
Softening life's edges
Filling me up again

It is just make-belief

I am still here
You are still gone

KNOWING

I miss being known

Words unspoken sitting between us
Because your arms already knew to hold me
Your lips already knew to rest upon my cheek

Now I must speak
A tired language
Words taste bitter and heavy
Crushing my tongue

You knew before I knew
Now no one knows

SILVER-LININGS

Not everything has a silver lining
Still, I look for the glittering edge
Of your dead body
Trying to recall
What silver even looks like

On days like these
I cannot remember
Anymore

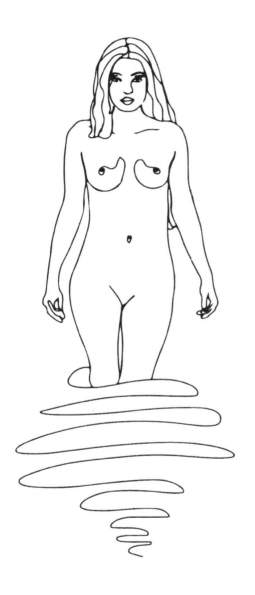

STRIP

They tell me
To tug on the thread
That binds me to you
If I pull it, they will see
When it unravels
I am left naked
Without you

ADDICT

A grief unhinged
    Rattling around in my chest
        Clawing at my organs
            Burying itself into my flesh

Opening old wounds
    Carving out new ones
        The thick red sludge seeps out
        Filling my lungs

I learn to breathe blood
    My alveoli coated in poison
        I become a masochist
            For the pain you left behind

        Addicted to anything
            That reminds me of you

CITIES

I have searched cities for you
Turning over sidewalk panels
Peering through dusty glass windows

I have waited in parks until midnight
Woken up with the crows

My soles bleed
My bones ache
My skin peels

But you never come

UPSIDE DOWN

There are 8 billion people in the world
You were the only one that made me feel like home
I felt whole inside your arms
Invincible with you by my side
I lost myself in you and did not even notice

I just was and we just were
Me merging into us, then into you
Two of you and none of me

Now that you are gone
I step back and see my whole world altered
I was unaware of the micro shifts
They happened in the breath between seconds

Now I realize I am living upside down
My moon is where the earth should be
Soil rains down from my sky
Coating my body in pallid brown

Eventually it will cover the ground beneath my feet
I will pull the stars up from their sunken soils
Carefully placing them back into the skies

I will rotate life back around
Until I am who I was before I met you

This time
Yes, this time
I will cement it in the universe

Never to be turned again

MAN OF HOLES

I paint snowflakes on the ceiling
To remind me of the day you left
As if these wounds were not already deep enough

My memories are not plastic
They do not sit idle
They are organic

Morphing
      Twisting
            Eroding

Each day I lose a little more of you
You are a man of holes

One day I will look at the ashes
Tucked neatly away in my closet
Wonder to myself

Who was this?

SHOULD'VE

I should have counted each touch
Stored each tender caress in a jar
With a violet lid
Keeping it on my shelf to peer into
When the nights are too cold
And my heart aches for warmth

SONG OF DECEMBER

I am already forgetting the melody of your life
The echo of the chords grows softer each day
Was your smile G-sharp or E-flat?
What was the tempo of your laugh?

I must remember!

Remember the ways our lives enmeshed
A beautiful concert of romance
My heartstrings pulling and weaving
The notes float into the air in a rhythmic dance

STARLIGHT

You can still see the light from a star that is dead

Maybe that is what people see
When they say they can see my light

They do not know that I have died long ago

WILDS

I could feel the ocean inside his touch
Hear galaxies with the beating of his heart
Catch fireflies in his mouth

The world may rest in the palms of another
But he gave me the universe

His shoes are so big
That an old Norse Troll could not fill
The footprints that he left behind on my heart

His touch so tender
That a wisp of cotton in the summer wind
Cannot match his soft caress

His laugh like sugar
Not even a cloud of honey bees
Could produce a tonic as sweet

The scales will always balance in his favor
He is the mark to which I measure a man

It is an unfair game
Rigged from the very start
You cannot win

I am left with only the memory of him
To keep me company
Even memory fades

One day I will be alone
With a ghost of a recollection

He is the only one with the key
To the wild garden
Growing inside my ribcage

I instead choose a loneliness
That will infest my hopes
Rot my heart

I choose an eternal heartache
Rather than to fall into anything
That is not his arms

A misery so sweet
That I would gladly drown
In my own foolishness
Rather than swim to any other shore

So, I will give my time, my smile, my touch
I will keep my heart and soul for him

For if he should ever return
Whatever is left of this tired unkempt heart
Will still beat for him

TRANSFORM

A little lipstick
A touch of lace
Curl your eyelashes
Straighten your hair

Transform yourself from a grieving widow
To someone no one has to think about anymore

THE DARK

I am back at the beginning
Sitting on the same day
When darkness came and settled in my life

Making its home inside me
Stealing food from my pantry
Sleeping in my bed
Leaving dirty dishes to wash

It has been a year
Still, the darkness eats dinner with me every night

When she leaves for a day or two
I leave a light on for her

My family asks why I leave on the light
Why not let darkness get lost and not find her way back?

It is because, I tell them, the darkness
Ties me to you

LOVERS

I am made nauseous by the love that grows around me
Husbands, wives, girlfriends, boyfriends, lovers, partners
My happiness for them has grown rancid
Spite drips like spoiled milk from my lips

I have grown jealous of the sun that lights their lives
Angry at the clouds that have hidden mine

If I cannot have my soulmate
Then no one else should have theirs
Let theirs be ripped away swiftly in the night

Without warning
Without reason

My mind a petty 3-year-old
Yearning for her favorite toy back
Stealing the toys of others on the playground
So that they, too, lose their joy

Feel the sting
The raw ache
The agonizing pain

Life is not a grade school playground
I must do better
Be better

I paint my lips a pale shade of plum
To color my fake smile

I listen to their love stories
Cackle at their lackluster tales
Nodding along like a wild woman

Then at night
I weep

ICE

Forever fixed in a glacier
That even a roaring fire cannot melt
Embers flying
Crackling and consuming

But maybe you could
Chisel me

TRAVEL

Grief follows me
Across oceans and channels
Up mountains and skyscrapers
Into the London Underground and to the top of the Eiffel Tower
On the canals of Amsterdam and through the patisseries of Paris
It waits for me at train stations and plane terminals
It rides the metro and eats ice cream
It lingers by my bedside to infect my dreams
Greeting me in the morning with poison kisses
Despite the miles crossed
Grief follows me

ANNOYANCES

I watch the movies you hated
Drink milk straight from the carton
Play the same song on repeat in the car
Leave closet doors ajar
Put extra spice into the curry
Order pizza with pineapple
Leave crumbs in the bed

All in the hopes that you will come back
Shake your head and stop me
I would hold your face in my palms
Kiss your nose gently
Whisper, "Sorry"
And undo it all

BLISS

I have attached my joy to you
You have taken off
Into the heavens
Pulling it with you
Just out of my reach

Part III
_____

SUMMER

TIME

They ask me how long it has been
I try to recall the days I have woken up without you

"Decades," I tell them

Then I remember the night the officer came to the door
I can recall every detail as it happened a moment ago

"Yesterday," I tell them

I count the holidays spent without you
Christmas, Easter, Birthdays,—hollowed out and filled with tears

"Years," I tell them

I recount the nights laying awake, my pillow soaked with tears
My breath stolen away from the heartache

"Centuries," I tell them

I think of the last time I felt safe resting in your arms
Matching my breath with yours and being one

"A Millennia," I tell them

WAIT

I am waiting
For the cracks in my bones to heal
I am waiting
For a new moon to howl to
I am waiting
For the memories to soften
I am waiting
For my heart to beat again

CHERRY TREE

The love we had was a fortress
A sea
A memory box
A cherry tree that we tended
It grew
And grew
When it blossomed
The petals covered the whole world
You cut down that tree when you left

I buried the branches with you

VOWS

Vows can be unstitched so easily
Swifter than I would have expected

      I have sat with the linen and threads in my hands
      For what feels like decades
      I cannot disentangle them from my flesh and bone
      From the fibers that once bound me to you

My grip has tightened around them so greatly
That I can feel my own pulse thumping in the palm of my hand
Beating to an unsteady tempo

      I have to let them go
      This I know
      "Not yet," I whisper to the trees
      "Not yet," they answer back

      Not. Yet.

GOODBYE

You went back to the earth today
The place from which you came

Born from the roots of the old Scots Pine
Covered in moss and ivy twisting its way to the sun

The tide will carry you out to the sea
You will travel the world on its wild currents

You were never mine to keep
I was only a burrower of your soft kisses

Your soul journeyed with mine for shorter than I needed
I am still learning to say goodbye

LINGER

If it was
"Till Death Do Us Part,"
How come I still feel you
Wherever I go?

HOME

The nest where we buried our treasure
and hid our dreams
is now gone.

The wind collapsed
what remained of it.

The sea has engulfed
each outstanding piece.

The days we built it
were long and hot.

Sweat beaded down our backs
as we sipped on cold tea
under the unforgiving sun.

We spent hours sorting
our collection of moss and twigs
gleaned from the forest floor.

Meticulously weaving the pieces
while stitching it together with hope.

A tedious creation
but ours nonetheless.

Every seashell and acorn had its place.

It was our fortress
to protect our tomorrows
and nurture our love.

When you left
the first stitch came undone.

Now our nest has unraveled
leaving wild scavengers to pluck
every last leaf and feather.

I sit alone under the stars
reminiscing about our citadel.

The cold night air stings
wrapping its talons around me.

The wind carries something from the East.
A white feather.

It floats and dances across the sky
before falling to the charred earth.

I reach for it
and cradle it in my hands.

I sit there for hours
being mesmerized by the soft lines.

The stars begin to dim
when someone calls my name from afar.
I know it is time to return home.

I tuck the feather into my coat pocket

Saving it for the day
when I begin again.

PRETEND

I am tired
    of pretending
        that there is light
where the darkness lives.

WAITING

I have seen wonders that pull tears of joy from world travelers
Touched statues that spark light into the hearts of mankind
Stood in stained glass cathedrals
Seen treasures hidden in the paint strokes from the past
Tasted delicacies that dance like fireflies on your tongue
Watched the sun rise over fields of lavender and set over white-water rivers
I have finished bucket lists and started new ones

> Yet, after all this I still wait
> Biding my time
> Until death finds me
> And brings me to you

FRACTURE

I am undoing you
Handing over the pieces
To others in my life

The Doctor
The Teacher
The Confidant
The Goofball
The Storyteller
The Listener
The Adventurer

Parts scattered
Yet, still remain

Once growing inside one heart
Now carried inside the ribs of many

CROW'S FEET

Remember my dear
When we danced in a rainbow of our making
Counting the ways
That we could make each other laugh

You carved out laugh lines on my cheeks
Left paint strokes in the crinkles of my eyes

I look in the mirror
And see you, still

These new grey hairs
The furrow between my brow
The lines running across my forehead
Burrowing in deep

All of it is your handiwork

There you are
Still leaving your mark

SUNSET

I still miss you
As clearly as the moon misses her stars
In the bright hours of the day

Though, she knows they will return
She only has to wait out the sun

CREASES

Take me
Fold me in half
Leave your crease
Across my heart
So that I can remember you
When you are gone

REST

Hold my soul for a moment
While I rest
Under the shade of the old plum tree
Away for the scorching sun
That beats down on my sunburnt neck
I promise that I will come back for it
When I awake
Then I will take my turn
Holding yours

SEASONS

The snow is coming
This I know
Summer will end
The leaves will golden, crinkle, and fall
The air will chill
The skies will open
Pour out its white powder
That will blanket the earth
Wiping the slate clean

Again

Turning this heart to ash

Again

Making me remember

Again

When the night wrapped you in her womb
Pulled you under the snowy waves of tranquility
Where your soul rests and mine breaks

Let summer stay forever

NOVEMBER

I carry the weight of November
Like a velvet cloak
Draped across my back
Slowing me down
Anchoring me in the past

DREAMS

When I dream of you
I sit in it for days
Reliving each moment
Curling into your touch
Memorizing each word
Holding on to you
For as long as possible
Eventually I have to let you go

I eagerly wait
For your return

ACQUAINTANCES

"He died?"

The words sit awkwardly on my computer screen
Old friends wondering, prying
Looking for confirmation

Their questions unsettle me

He has not left
He lives on the other side of the curtain that I cannot cross
At least not yet

He is the air, the sun, and the stars
The golden leaves adorning the trees in autumn
The first cherry blossom when spring is awakening
The kaleidoscope of snowflakes falling in the January sky

He is here
He will forever be here

I delete the message and close my laptop
Feeling the warmth of his smile upon me

REWIND

Tick tock, tick tock, tick . . .
. . . Then she stops
– the watch –
That counts down to death

Now your soul rests
In an endless sleep
Wrapped up in the sheets
Of eternity

As you left
You took the moon
Stole the stars
Venus and Mars
Tucked into your back pocket

You left me in pitch black
Even the crack of dawn
Has fled
I asked God to put them back
Please, my love
Resist the night
Bring back my light

"But they are his now", God said
No! No! They were *mine*!
I watched them shimmer and shine
Lighting my sky
They were never yours to take
Now I am wrapped in an eternal night

PEARLS

I am here
I float on the string of pearls that you left for me
Dancing down the glimmering spheres
Moving to the melodies
That draw me closer in time with you
Floating
Falling
Gracefully pirouetting
To a destiny that you seemed to know
More about than me

POSSIBILITY

A world

    Of endless possibilities

But all I want

    Is you

Part IV

AUTUMN

BLOOM

I beckon the morning
After nights of feasting on sorrow
The light fills the pieces left by the scavengers
Hunting and gathering in the hollows of my heart

I leave it open for them to take
As I have hidden away the best fragments
Growing a garden in the ashes of my soul
That will blossom in spring

COUNT

I count my breaths
With the rise and fall of my chest
In and out
Until I lose myself in the count
Between reality and wherever I am
That is where I rest
Until the moon emerges
And the fear passes

CONSTERNATION

If you were here
You would know what to say
When the fear becomes too loud

You would know what to do
When my bones shake with panic

You would know how to console
The worry in my chest

Alas, you are not

I must learn
How to quiet the storm
Finding ways to make peace
With the tempest

ONWARDS

I wake up
The smell of you is distinctively missing
The sweet touch of your lips on my skin
As you whisper "Good Morning" into my neck
Has twisted into a memory that I cling to

The cool draft coming from your side of the bed
Infiltrates my game of make-belief
In which I am a lonesome wife
With a husband working away

I am learning to set the table for one
I am learning to march onwards

I am learning
That forward does not mean forgetting

LITTLE JOYS

You took away my telescope
Yet, I can still see the constellations outside my window
Making wishes on the stars that you left in my sky

I can chase the feeling of joy that you put into my heart

In the first bite of a chocolate cake
In pink skies at night
In wearing short skirts and making big plans
In a dollop of cold whipped cream on a warm apple pie
In finding the perfect shade of berry lipstick
In long walks under the moonlit sky
In a warm casserole on a cold February night
In duvet forts and pillow shacks

Yes, my dear
I can still feel you in the world around me

GALAXY

Hand in hand
We flew across the universe
Choosing the best pieces of each world
Making a mosaic to call home

I have been picking up the pieces
That you left behind

I am tired and worn
Following after you

I think it is time
I dig up my roots
Shake off my wings
Create a galaxy of my own

DREAMER

I am still a dreamer
Despite the dreams you emptied
I can feel the magic that steeps and brews
When the world sleeps
I lay awake in the stillness of the night
Listening to the tempo of the darkness
The moon laughing from her perch in the sky

TENDER

He loved me tenderly
Holding my broken pieces
Kissing the jagged edges
Even though they cut his lips
He never tried to put those pieces
Back together

I was not a puzzle
I was a mosaic
For him, that was enough

SENSES

Time stains my memory
I unravel scrolls
Hoping to catch a glimpse of your smile
All I see is smudges where your eyes should be

    I wonder how much longer
    Until the pain replaces all that is left of you

Then I hear your song on the radio
Smell your cologne
Taste your favorite candy

    I remember again

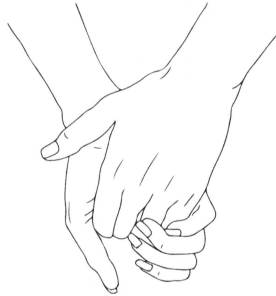

FLY

There will come a day
When we will fly again
I will take your hand
Interlock your fingers in mine
Feel the pulse of our hearts beating between our palms
I will look at you and smile
Knowing
It was worth the wait

INFERNO

I am never going to let my wings be clipped again
My Medusa strangled
My life song muted

Never again
Will I allow a man to make his home
Inside my throne room

My colors will never be stripped
Or my light dimmed right before the crack of dawn
I will let my light shine through the day
Merging with the rings of Saturn

I will be constellations
I will be galaxies

I do not need them gifted to me
I would rather make my own sunshine
Laboring until the early hours of morning

Than to accept a ray of gold from the mouth of a lover
Spinning and weaving their magic into me
Only to pull out poisonous thorns

I am inhospitable to man
My fire burns too hot
My flame gouging out the darkness
Leaving blisters on soft hands
Burning through linens, scorching lace

I have always turned down my flame
To welcome them in

This time
I will crank the heat
Burn the nations to the ground
From their calloused soils
I will watch new life grow

BITTER

Time away from you
Tastes like burnt coffee
Still, I drink it
Waiting for it to turn into
A honey-wine

WILDLY

You loved me wildly

And left me

To try to find love again

In a world

Of tame hearts

WIDOWS

Two souls
Well acquainted with death
Coming together for coffee

To gossip
About how they escaped
The Devil's grasp

To find life
Beyond the darkness

CONTEMPLATIONS

I have been smoothing out the creases
Of my crumpled heart
Weaving together the frayed edges
Ironing the folds

I can still see the day that you left
Branded with fire
In the middle of my heart

> Yet, I feel pride at the thing
> That still beats inside my chest

Now, I must decide:
Do I unfold my rib cage once more?
Risking fire, monsoon, earthquake, and abandonment

> Are these bones a fort keeping my heart safe?
> Or are they a prison to keep love out?

KISMET

I think of the way we loved each other
Two fractured hearts stitched together
In hopes of finding an anchor
In the rhythm of the others heartbeat

        Spinning magic from moonlit bays
        Saving jars of hope for a rainy day
        Finding stardust in sidewalk cracks
        That is what our love was

DAYBREAK

Looking back
I see a great expanse
Between the place where you left me
And where I am now

Miles stretch out behind me
I feel the warmth of the rising sun upon my cheeks
The stars are still out, dancing lightly in the sky

Some days I run towards the sun
Slowly emerging on the horizon
Its yellow glow beckoning me forward

Other days I stop in my tracks
Sit down
Cross-legged
Weeping for the distance between us

Sometimes I even walk back towards you
Picking up rocks as I go
Feeling them heavy in my pockets

Even so the distance grows
I lose more rocks than I can pick up
I fill the emptiness with wildflowers

RISK

I ask my heart
So tender and tired
If she thinks we can risk again

She whispers back tales
Of feathered joy and amber love

Yet, I wonder if one step forward
Is worth the risk
Of three steps back

DRAGON

I am awakening
To the whispers of the New
That have called to me
From before I was born
I am finally listening

Breathing in the lessons
Breathing out fire

FREEDOM

I am pleased for you my dear
You are in a place where magic is born
Light enfolds each atom of your being
You are free

Your demons cannot find you where you are
No longer must you be brave and strong
You can sink into the caverns of love
Where all your wounds will heal into scars

They tell me it was selfish of you to leave
Though who can resist the call of all-consuming love?
The glimmer of eternal peace is irresistible
This I know

And so, my love
I rest in the thought of you
With your newly budded wings
Soaring with the comets and gliding on sunbeams

TOMORROW

Send me the petals
That they scattered on your grave
Let me sew them into a ribbon
That will float across the stars
To remind me of the journey
That lead me to a place
Where tomorrow is not as scary
As it was yesterday

DELECTATION

Joy is in the little things

This is something I once knew
Yet, had forgotten

A cup of earl grey tea
A Sunday afternoon nap
A fresh pot of coffee
A first kiss
A second kiss
Brunch with friends
Puppy cuddles
The last sentence of a book
Finding something once lost

Yes, joy is still here
Hiding in the wrinkles of life

HESITANCY

My heart knows the fragility in its tempo
Letting me know to go slow

Sometimes my heart beckons me
To yield to the new
To hold back
To retreat

I ask my heart what she needs
She whispers that all she wants
Is the feeling that you took when you left

I tell her we can find it again
She warns of the hope that comes
Before the heartbreak

MME. PAIN

When pain has a heartbeat
You know the thing that lives within you
Once a hatchling
Has become a beast
Tenfold grown

When pain has a cry
You learn to silence her shrieks
Letting her feed on jam and joy
From the bottom of the trunk
That you keep her in

When pain has a song
That she teaches you at night
You find yourself humming it
To fill the silence
When everyone who said
That they would stay
Has left

Then pain tells you
She has a secret
That she promises to show you
When you keep her in
And others out

You have a choice

To keep feeding her
Loving her
Holding her
Or you open up the trunk
Where she roams
You let her out
And tell her
To go live in someone else

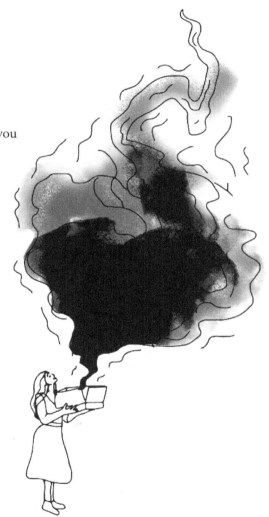

GARDEN

I am ready to begin
Planting seeds
Nourishing the soil

Clearing the weeds
That have smothered my heart
Clamping down on my dreams

The toil does not frighten me
As I have lived a thousand nightmares

I am ready to create
My own daydreams
With fairies, love spells . . .

. . . and husbands that stay

OCTOBER 31

Eating Halloween candy alone
On a couch made for two
Remembering your silly smile
When I put on my witch hat
Lips painted in black
Dark shadow smeared across my eyes
I took out the kitchen broom
Held it out for you
You hopped on
And we flew to the moon

ENCHANTMENT

You were fairy dust
In a world that had forgotten magic

GRIEF ATTACK

The biting edge of grief
Swarms around me again

Sinking its talons back in
Just when I thought I had fled
From its anchored grip

Clipped breath
Jagged Heart

Hope pulled away
Waiting again
For this all to fade
And for life
To come back in

NEW LOVER

Treat me gently
Do not pull at my tattered edges

Hold me

Whisper sonnets
Into my darkness

Stoke my fire with kindness
Leave your sharpness at the door

When you enter
Come in slowly

Crawl steadily towards my heart

HUNTER

I can see the forest now
After spending years among the wild pine
Hunting for loves return

The light never did shine in those woods
The earth is cold and unforgiving
The wind leaves its burn upon my lips

The earth cradling my feet is rusted
The canopy above is molding
The poison air constricts my lungs

I overstayed my time here
When I emerge with swollen eyes and blistered tongue
I shall make my new home among the waves

GIFT

Now I can finally see
That loving you was a gift
Given and then taken
Forever etched into my heart

SOMNOLENCE

Creeping towards another shoreline
Wondering how much longer
Before the waves roll me back to a slumber
Taking me to a place
Where gardens still grow
And morning follows the night

SURRENDER

I give in to the forces that skulk in the night
Sinking into what I once ran from

I learn tales of heartache and triumph here
Etching each lesson into my collapsing heart
Taking them with me when the time turns
And I am released from this place
Of lamenting creatures and wounds that weep

Finally discovering hidden truths
Giving in does not have to be giving up

PERSPECTIVE

I chisel a fortress into the cliffs
That I have failed to summit

The passage North is taxing
I have made the attempt countless times

I learn to make friends with the monsters
Living in the mountain depths

Finding pieces of solitude in a place
Where shadows once roamed

GRATITUDE

Some days I try to forget you
Sending your memory
To the soft edges
Of my mind

Unraveling you
From the pulp and flesh
Of my heart

You always come back
In thoughts
In dreams
In words of those who loved you

I am pushed into remembering
Pushed to feeling it all again
Awakening wounds
That I had tucked in to bed

Turning over soils
Where I planted the stars
That would light the trail
To a new tomorrow

So, I remember
Learning to find gratitude
In the echoes of your life

GROWTH

Tease out these insecurities
The things that he forgot to take with him
Like the pounding thoughts
Of fallen stars
And lackluster wishes

Melt down the idiosyncrasies
In a porcelain crucible
Gather the remnants

Let them be a reminder
Of the darkness that once was
So that I never again
Grow accustomed to the light

BLEND

He was so young
And so was I
Two fawns lost in the woods
Call me Bambi
    Now I think of the road ahead
    Years and years and years and years
    To be lived; to be survived
        Would I be gifted another?
        To keep me company along the way
        Lending colors
        Making purple
            Or is life to be red, crimson, maroon?
            Monotone and flat
            I can only ask
            Waiting for the road to whisper back

HEAL

Bathe me in juniper
Wrap me in linens weaved by Mother Earth
Let me feast on mint and milk
Call to the midnight ravens
Tell them to sing over my soul
For when I rise
I will not return
To the caverns below

SHADOW

I see you shadow
Sticky and sulking
Waxing then waning
Ready to devour the light

I no longer feed you
A banquet of heartache
Saving you scraps
From my nights in the valley

I will offer you tonics of joy
Light from the source
Wisdom from the earth

You will purge out the dark
To let in the daylight

DIVE

I make bets with the universe
Double dog daring
Drop me further in
Let me sink
Until I hit the bottom of the ocean
Then let me dive further

    Down

        Down

            Down

                I am not afraid
                Because I know it is at the bottom
                Where the wisdom lies
                Where my wings are formed
                Where the scabs peel
                Where the wounds heal

EPILOGUE

THERE HAS BEEN NO grand dissolution of grief in my life. There are days that are still agonizing and days that are unremarkably stale. I can say that the one difference from where I was during the 'winter' days of grief, to where I am in 'autumn', is the fact that I have trudged through the wild thickets of sorrow. I have endured the sleepless nights, the months of not eating and of eating too much, of crying in an empty bed until the sun awakens, and being carried home by darkness at the end of the day. I have restricted life; I have overindulged in life. I have wept, I have cursed, and I have screamed into the great chasm of mourning.

I found that time does not heal all wounds—I have to work each day towards healing. Sometimes healing work looks like showering and putting on clean clothes, other times it is reading a book on grief, reaching out to a friend, or going to therapy. Even after the passage of time, there are still days when the pain rears up and shakes my heart once more. On these days, I sink into grief and rest in the familiar feelings of sorrow. There can be comfort there. Yet, I know I cannot stay there too long and I must climb out of the suffocating lair of sadness where air is restricted along with life.

Each day I am greeted with the choice to drink the tonics of heartache or brew up my own pot of joy. Some days I gulp down the juice of sadness and sit in the past for a while. Holidays, anniversaries, and birthdays often require a few pitchers of heartache. I watch the world continue on around me in a bustling haze that makes me wonder how everyone keeps going, and yet, on other days I become one of those wonderous moving figures. The strength I have gathered from the days of tears and torment has gifted me the ability to crawl out of that grief cavern and continue moving onward. And so, I trek on towards the rising sun, collecting memories to bring with me to show my late husband when I meet him on the otherside.

GRIEF RESOURCES

IF YOU HAVE EXPERIENCED the loss of a loved one, know that you are not alone. If you are feeling overwhelmed with grief, it is okay to ask for support and reach out to someone you trust. Below is a list of some resources that have been created to support grievers on their journey to healing.

My Grief
mygrief.ca
Mygrief.ca was developed by families and grief experts in order to help you to understand and work through your grief. It includes resources from professionals and stories from people who have experienced loss. It is confidential and can be accessed in the privacy of your own home.

What's Your Grief?
whatsyourgrief.com
What's Your Grief was created by two mental health professionals with 20+ years of experience in grief and bereavement. The website provides general educational information from mental health professionals, including articles, webinars, and e-courses.

Grief Share
griefshare.org
Grief Share is a grief recovery support group led by people who understand what you are going through. There are Grief Share support groups throughout Canada and the US, and ten others countries. Check out their website to find a group near you.

Grief Recovery Method
griefrecoverymethod.com
The Grief Recovery Method is a heart-centered, action-oriented, and evidenced-based approach that helps grievers deal with the pain of emotional loss in any relationship. The program offers tangible tools that help you move through your grief. The website can help you find a Grief Recovery Method specialist in your area.

Refuge in Grief
refugeingrief.com
Refuge in Grief is an online community and resource that helps people who are grieving. The creator, Megan Devine, is a psychotherapist, writer, and grief advocate who shares podcasts, online courses, and other grief literature.

Psychology Today
psychologytoday.com
Psychology Today is a portal where you can look up grief therapists in your city as well as access different tools and resources to help you understand and work through your grief.

Terrible, Thanks for Asking
ttfa.org
Terrible, Thanks for Asking is a podcast hosted by Nora McInerny. The podcast asks people to share their complicated and honest feelings about how they really are, including discussion of grief and loss.

Soaring Spirits International
soaringspirits.org
Soaring Spirits is an inclusive, non-denominational organization focused on hope and healing through the grieving process. They offer tools and resources for rebuilding your life in the aftermath of the loss of a life partner.

Spark of Life
sparkoflife.org
Spark of Life offers grief coaching, online courses, and grief retreats. Their mission is to provide a supportive, safe, restorative environment for grieving hearts to find hope and healing.

SUICIDE PREVENTION AND
MENTAL HEALTH RESOURCES

IF YOU OR SOMEONE you love is experiencing suicide ideation or struggling with their mental health, know that you are not alone and there are tools and resources to help. I encourage you to reach out to someone you trust, and find a professional mental health care provider. You do not have to walk through this alone. There are people who care about you and want to help. You are deserving and worthy of support.

Center for Suicide Prevention
Suicideinfo.ca
The Center for Suicide Prevention's website offers videos, webinars, statistics, in-depth editorial articles, infographics, and other suicide prevention resources.

Mind Your Mind
mindyourmind.ca
Mind Your Mind is a space where mental health, wellness, engagement, and technology meet. They work with community partners and young people to co-create interactive tools and innovate resources.

Your Life Counts
yourlifecounts.org
Your Life Counts provides numbers and contact information for mental health services while providing extensive resources on mental health.

Help Guide
helpguide.org
Help Guide can assist you in finding mental health resources, including information on suicide prevention, depression, and grief.

Psychology Today
psychologytoday.com
Psychology Today is an online portal where you can look up mental health therapists in your city as well as access different tools and resources.

The Jack Project
jack.org
The Jack Project unites young people by focusing on ending the stigma attached to mental health issues. Since stigma is often the central reason that stops people from getting the help they need, Jack's motto of 'No more silence' sends a strong message.

IMAlive
imalive.org
IMAlive is a virtual crisis center. It offers volunteers who are trained in crisis intervention. These individuals are ready to instant message with anyone who needs immediate support.

The Trevor Project
thetrevorproject.org
The Trevor Project offers crisis intervention and suicide prevention to LGBTQ youth through its hotline, chat feature, text feature, and online support center.

Veterans Crisis Line
Veteranscrisisline.net
The Veterans Crisis Line is a free, confidential resource staffed by qualified responders from the Department of Veterans Affairs. Anyone can call, chat, or text—even those not registered or enrolled with the VA.

Befrienders
befrienders.org
Befrienders is a global network of 349 emotional support centers around the world. It offers an open space for anyone in distress to be heard. Support is available via telephone, text message, in person, online, and through outreach and local partnerships.

Suicide Stop

suicidestop.com

Suicide Stop is an online source for emergency numbers, online chats, suicide hotlines and therapy options.

Other supports in your community may include:

- Your physician
- Community and private counselors
- Employee Assistance Programs
- Community programs
- Emergency and short-term stay shelters
- Trusted family and friends

NOTE FROM THE AUTHOR

IF YOU ARE LOOKING for a sign that you need to get additional support or help, this is it. If you or someone you know is experiencing suicidal thoughts or behavior, please seek the support of a mental health professional. Do not wait.

You matter. You are loved.
The world is a better place because you are in it.

Made in the USA
Monee, IL
02 April 2021

64406251R00085